There is Elevation in Loss

How the pain of grief becomes the path to purpose

by

Vanessa Andrieux

2nd Edition

© 2024, 2025 Guided to Glory, LLC
All rights reserved. No part of this book may be reproduced in any form without permission from the author, except for the use of quotations in a book review. For more information, address: info@beguidedtoglory.com

The content in this book is for informational purposes only and does not constitute medical, psychological, or other professional advice. The author and publisher disclaim any responsibility for any liability, loss, or risk, personal or otherwise, incurred directly or indirectly as a consequence of the use or application of any information contained in this book.

Library of Congress Cataloging in Publication Data
Registration Number: TXu 2-441-448
246 Robert C Daniel Jr Pkwy
Augusta, GA 30909

First Edition: 2024
Second Edition: 2025 (Expanded and Revised).

Previously edited by Mozelle Jordan
Proofed and edited by K. Faison
Cover photo inspired by Crystal Beard
featuring the author,
Vanessa Andrieux
Photographed by J.D. Williams
Printed in the United States of America

ISBN 979-8-9918001-0-5 Paperback
ISBN 979-8-9918001-1-2 eBook Edition
(This ISBN was originally assigned to the 1st edition.)
Second Edition (Revised and Expanded), 2025
This updated edition includes new chapters, restructured content, and additional reflections by the author.

Contents

PREFACE	3
1 EMBRACING AUTHENTICITY	7
2 FROM SILENCE TO EMPOWERMENT	15
3 REDEFINING SUCCESS	23
4 THE JOURNEY OF "I DO"	31
5 BEHIND CLOSED DOORS	49
6 OPTING FOR CHANGE	57
7 FACING REALITY	65
8 FROM PAIN TO POWER	73
9 FINDING RESILIENCE	79
10 THE RETURN	91
11 RISING TO THE OCCASION	99
12 NAVIGATING TRANSITIONS	103
13 A TURN TOWARD HAPPILY, EVER AFTER…	107
14 THE POWER OF SURRENDER	119
15 FROM MY HEART TO YOURS	131
ACKNOWLEDGEMENTS	137
APPENDIX	141

Preface

I begin by acknowledging that the events that unfolded in my life have guided me here. I've learned to appreciate every piece of my story, recognizing that, ultimately, God orchestrates our story for his glory and for the greater good of those around us.

I am a huge advocate for prioritizing mental health to break the chains of generational curses. Investing in ourselves is not a luxury; it is a personal responsibility that encompasses us as a whole. As active participants in society, our self-care has a direct impact on the way we inspire those around us. Let us contribute to the collective uplifting of one another.

Every loss and gain in my life has left an unforgettable mark. It has instilled in me the determination to love more deeply, work harder, and savor every aspect of life with newfound appreciation. Our time on Earth is limited. It is a gift, not to be taken for granted. When we compromise on what we know is wrong, we experience less of what God has for us. Choose alignment with His will because that is where true peace and purpose lie. Spread love, grant forgiveness, and release yourself from the shackles that have you stuck. Stand up for your convictions and dedicate yourself to developing your mind, body, and soul. If you do not know how, ask the Lord Jesus Christ to show you the way, and HE will deliver. We have been given the power to choose.

There is Elevation in Loss may not be for everyone, but for those it speaks to, I pray that it provides a piece of what you need to break free. Dad, as I cared for you during your last days with us, I told you I would make the sacrifices you and Mom made count, and I pray that I do. I love you.

1

Embracing Authenticity

What happens when you grow up believing you are not enough? How do you learn to love yourself when the world first taught you not to? For me, the answer took years to uncover. I was that person — I did not like myself very much growing up. I was the girl who felt overlooked and unheard: the overweight, glasses-wearing Black girl with crooked teeth and a messed-up relaxer. In the 90s, what was depicted as beautiful were slim, fair-skinned girls with pin-straight hair and perfectly white teeth. Watching these women in almost every movie, TV show, and magazine led me to believe that I was not pretty enough to be anyone significant in the world. As I grew older, this lowered my self-esteem. Over the years, it reached a point where I found ways to be anyone but myself. I was too insecure to date traditionally, so in middle school, I began online dating. While this seems completely normal now, in the early 2000s, it was not as popular as it is today. Online dating allowed me to conceal my identity. *No one I am interested in can see my flaws, so let's start here,* I thought. Little did I know that it was the beginning of heartbreak that would last for years to come.

While creating my online profiles, I pretended to be other girls —the ones depicted by mainstream media as beautiful. I used pictures of women that looked as close to that depiction as possible and passed them off as myself. I got into several casual relationships that way, but the last and final time I did this, I met a guy I fell in love with.

At that time in my life, he was everything I thought I wanted in a man: older, more mature, established, and super attractive. So, while still in high school and before ever meeting in person, we got into a serious, committed, long-distance relationship that lasted four years. I did not reveal my identity to him until a couple of years into our relationship. After a couple of years of hiding my physical appearance, I broke down and told him the truth about who I was. To my surprise, he said he still wanted to give "us" a try and asked if we could finally meet in person. The summer before we met, I embarked on a weight-loss journey, losing over 100 pounds. When I returned to school for junior year, people barely recognized me. Classmates swore I had weight-loss surgery or took weight-loss supplements to achieve my goal, but if they only knew I lost those 100 pounds through diet and exercise alone! Although I was impressed with myself because I looked slim, I still struggled with insecurities. It was hard to wrap my mind around my new image, my new body. My best friend witnessed times when I would look in the mirror, trying to hide the areas of my body I felt were not slim enough, partly because excess skin was the result of my weight loss. I talked negatively about my size, wanting to lose more weight. My best friend said I suffered from body dysmorphia then, and hey, maybe she was right.

In March, my boyfriend flew from Oregon to Miami to meet me. We spent a few days together, he met my family, and everything seemed to be going well. I thought that this was going to be the start of something beautiful! This was our chance to start over. I was mortified by the lie I had told him. I had betrayed him for years and could not understand why he decided to give us a second chance. I was head over heels in love and thrilled to have another opportunity for us to be together. When he flew back to Oregon, emotional distance grew between us. We were not on the phone late at night with each other, and we would often go for days without speaking. I started to feel him pull away.

Apparently, he had become close with a woman he met through one of his friends, and as their friendship progressed, our relationship deteriorated. Eventually, he stopped replying to my messages and calls altogether, never to be seen or heard from again. It wrecked me. But then again, I thought to myself, *Vanessa, what did you really expect?* A part of me knew that his decision to give us a second chance was too good to be true, but when our relationship ended, I was ruined. I thought I would never recover from this break-up. Even though our relationship ended, this challenge led me to discover my passion for health and wellness; it unknowingly set the stage for my profound personal growth.

Self-care became a top priority, leading me to adopt a routine of working out six days a week. Physical fitness and nourishing my body were my new favorite topics. This journey was both exhilarating and a revelation that taught me to tune into what my body needed to stay healthy. However, self-doubt still plagued me from my past weight. It was difficult for me to appreciate the strides I had made in improving my health. It took years to acknowledge my progress and to live confidently in my new body.

I was on an emotional roller coaster, trying to accept who the 'new' me was, but it was as if my body and mind were at war with each other. I did not learn this until later, but I now know that I had entered something referred to as weight-loss grief, and overcoming this grief was complex. I was experiencing grief marked by struggles with loose skin, the pressure to maintain my new weight, ambiguous comments, and a whirlwind of new attention.

Since I was a young girl, and even after losing weight, I struggled with my relationship with food. Hidden binge eating sessions and a silent battle with food restrictions were my reality for years, long before I could name these experiences as disorders. I snuck food out of the kitchen and found comfort in eating, even when I was not hungry. This struggle created an unhealthy relationship with food, causing my weight to fluctuate for years.

God works in mysterious ways, though. After I became a licensed practical nurse, I was led to a position as a Recovery Coach at a residential eating disorder facility. There, I witnessed the struggles of individuals across the spectrum of eating disorders, from anorexia to bulimia, ranging from teenagers to older women. I offered empathy from my experience with struggling with food, allowing me to relate to them in ways that I could tell were impactful. Being present for them unexpectedly kick-started my healing journey with food, teaching me to honor my body's needs, recognize my hunger cues, and reflect on how I felt before and after each meal. This is when I truly recognized that my body deserves proper care and respect. I can admit that I was harder on myself than anyone else ever was. Even though I was my worst critic, I knew I was loved. I did not give anyone a chance to be there for me during this season in my life, but embracing these truths in my adulthood enabled me to start treating myself kindly. This shift marked the beginning of whole-body healing. I've come to see that as humans, we are inherently imperfect, make mistakes, face limitations, and are always learning. We crave love, acceptance, and connection, both from those around us and from ourselves. I began to understand that we can leverage pain to improve our lives, a lesson I am eager to pass forward

2

From Silence to Empowerment

My parents are my heroes for so many reasons. The level of sacrifice they made to leave Haiti to settle in the United States, where opportunities are abundant, is something I will forever appreciate. My mom and dad invested everything they had in our family. They both worked full-time in the evenings, losing precious time with their children. Because of this, when I was a child, my oldest brother and sister raised my brother and me. Even in my parents' absence, I admired who they were; my mom was my dad's rock, the pillar of support and coordinator of the home, and my dad was the kind of father who, although he did not remember my birthday and was not the one to take me to the doctor or come to my school events, I knew he was there when I needed him. My dad would cook on occasion, but for most of our home meals, it was my mom who did the cooking. I did not get to see my parents when I got home from school, but I knew dinner would be ready when I arrived and that one of my oldest siblings would be home to care for us.

I grew up in an authoritarian household. Both my father and mother had clear, high expectations of us. My mom was softer than my dad, but she allowed him to parent us the best way he saw fit. We were not allowed to question authority, and speaking when we were not spoken to was out of the question. Voicing an opinion contrary to an adult was considered disrespectful. We were expected to have close to perfect attendance, make good grades, stay out of trouble, and maintain a clean house without question. Yes, my parents were strict with their rules, but deep down, I knew these rules were established to equip us for our future.

As a young girl who already felt unaccepted, being scolded as a child meant I failed. As a result, failure was almost impossible to navigate. It was difficult for me to accept helpful criticism as I got older because I strived for perfection. I wanted my parents to be proud of me, so I strived to please them by performance. Since I was so focused on being the best version of myself for them, my self-discovery was delayed.

There were a few places I would hang out in my childhood where I felt like I could get what I was missing from home. My best friend's house was one of the places. I slept over there as often as I could because I felt like my emotions were valid there, unlike at home. I felt that her family was more present than mine because my parents were often working. Whether I was sleeping at her house or she was sleeping at mine, I knew that if we were together, we would have a blast. This helped alleviate the stressors I felt with being at home.

The other place was my older cousin's house on my dad's side. Whenever I was there, I felt heard. She somehow always knew how to make me feel better. Her kind words, good food, and warm conversations drew me in regularly. Her house was also the meeting place for our cousins, but I discovered more insecurities when I went to her house. During my middle school years, I was over 250 pounds and struggling with my self-image. Although I felt love and support at her house, I did not feel fully accepted by my cousins. I felt like I was not cool enough to be in what I labeled in my head as the "cool cousin crew" because I was the odd, semi-nerdy, overweight, heavy-breathing cousin who wore glasses.

I was aware of the love, safety, and security my parents provided for us at home, but the expectations set for me as a child were high. Life, oftentimes, felt stressful. It was easy to bring the same high demands from home with me wherever I went. Carrying high expectations with me into adulthood left me, in essence, being hard on myself.

In my early twenties, my mom helped me get my first job in the medical field. She had been employed there for about 20 years, so I knew I had a foot in with her connections. I was excited to begin working in the emergency department as a phone operator and later as a secretary at the ripe age of 18, but I was not sure if I would fare well in my position. Growing up, I was taught to hold leaders in high regard, so I developed a fear of interacting with authority figures at this level. The thought of how they would react if I made a mistake filled me with dread, causing me to cave under pressure. As I faced tough situations at work, I learned that I was not being heard because I was not speaking up. I knew I could not remain silent and become an effective woman in society simultaneously.

   I came to accept that the part of me that battled using my voice was underdeveloped and recognized that I had to forgive my parents for silencing me as a child. I decided to acknowledge that they raised me to the best of their abilities. If I wanted to navigate life successfully and develop meaningful relationships, I would have to cultivate this part of myself. Fast forward to adult life, I began therapy and started the process of discovering my boundaries, learning what I would accept and what I could no longer tolerate in both my personal and professional life. I began speaking up and learning how to feel confident, demanding space when I walked into a room.

I loved going to school as a child, but I was bullied throughout elementary and middle school because of my size. This led to many unprocessed emotions, but I learned during this time that writing helped me release some of them. I love to write, so picking up journaling during my childhood felt natural. I started journaling at a young age, and it has remained a powerful outlet. As I grew older, I would write out positive affirmations and set personal goals. I learned to prioritize self-care, which has helped me grow more confident in who I am becoming.

After putting in the work to improve myself, I felt like I deserved more than to stay quiet. I felt, with conviction, that my voice was important and should be heard. If I did not speak up for myself, who would? After all these years, I developed my sense of self, and sure, it took me a while to get comfortable with speaking without fear of judgment, but I had finally reached a place in my life where I knew my thoughts and opinions mattered; if it did not matter to anyone but me, that was enough.

When I became a parent, I knew that there were aspects of raising children I would use from my parents, like instilling respect, integrity, and perseverance in my children. I knew that I would impart some of what I did not receive as well. I did not want to create the same dynamic of feeling unheard or invalidated that I experienced when I was growing up. I learned through my own parenting journey that if we let our children's voices be heard, it can increase their self-esteem and trust in us. This will ultimately help them cultivate the confidence to speak up for themselves.

Throughout my childhood, my mother and I nurtured a close bond. She was the parent I could confide in without the fear of authoritarian discipline, and I deeply appreciated having this type of relationship with her. It was not until I got older that my dad and I grew closer, and I could enjoy him more outside of his authoritative role, finally seeing more of his sense of humor and weaknesses. My dad and I developed a better relationship when I became an adult. I believe it's because my dad got to see his hard work pay off. He saw me flourish into a responsible, respectful, successful adult, and here, we thrived.

3

Redefining Success

I have learned over the years that the definition of success is subjective. To some, success may mean achieving financial wealth. To others, it may mean fame, owning material possessions, or professional growth. Whichever way you choose to define success, one version does not supersede the other. Success is not just about physical achievements. The day we start valuing peace, purpose, and authenticity over possessions and titles, our society will reach a new level of fulfillment.

My definition of success has changed over the years. I used to think success meant following the same path my parents did—meet someone, fall in love, get married, build a family, work hard, and live a stable life together. I set out with that exact plan, but life had a different plan for me, one that taught me success is not about recreating someone else's story—it's about growing through your own.

Situations in life started to happen beyond my control; I could not quite understand why things were not working out the way I wanted. Weren't things going well a moment ago? I started to question whether I was truly living by my own purpose—or just following someone else's idea of what they believed my purpose should be.

Straight out of high school, my mom helped me land a job at the hospital where she worked. I began college that same summer. I knew I wanted to practice Nursing since high school, so that was my primary focus. However, it was not easy to obtain. It seemed easy for my colleagues at the hospital, yet I could not understand why. It was like everywhere I looked, someone was earning their Registered Nurse license. Some were being accepted into traditional Bachelor's in Nursing programs, while others quickly gained entry into accelerated nursing programs.

Determined to find an alternative way to obtain my nursing license after being rejected by several universities, I attended a community college, where I earned an associate's degree. While taking my prerequisite courses, I failed microbiology, a requirement for admission to the bachelor's degree program in nursing. Although I failed this course, I was not going to allow that to deter my plan. I had my future mapped out. I wanted to obtain a bachelor's degree, and I was driven to see my plan through to completion.

I received an Associate's Degree in Nursing, then applied to a Licensed Practical Nursing program, followed by an RN accelerated program. I graduated from Mercy Hospital College of Nursing with a second Associate's Degree. Even though it was not part of my initial plan, it was one of the happiest times in my life because I persevered. After I passed my board exam and received my license, I felt uncertain about what my career as a nurse would look like. I thought, "*What am I supposed to do with this?*"

    I felt accomplished when I held my nursing license; I could not have been prouder of myself. When I previously worked at the hospital as a secretary, I witnessed the high stress levels, lengthy shifts, and heavy workload the nurses had, so I would pursue a nursing job that offered a better work-life balance. Although I did not have a bachelor's degree, getting this nursing license was something I needed to achieve.

    Receiving recognition from my loved ones after graduating from the RN program was a huge deal for me. I wanted them to be proud of me. It reminded me that I am a conqueror as I consistently found a way to remain dedicated to my goal. Whenever I thought, 'Did I do all of this just to possibly not use this nursing license I worked so hard to get?' I would quickly counter that with, "*Absolutely not!*" I love helping people, and with a nursing license, I get to do that. As I attempted to discover how I would use my nursing license, I realized there are many ways to make a living as a nurse; that I did not have to become a clinical nurse if my heart was not in it. After I moved to Augusta, by the grace of God, I found an amazing job with minimal clinical work involved.

Finally, I secured a job in my nursing career, but life taught me that achieving a goal alone is not the definition of success. It is essential to remember that reaching our goals do not mean our desires stop there. Having new ambitions is human nature, and ultimately, part of what makes us successful is adaptability. If the desire to achieve a new goal arises, consider exploring it.

In our spiritual lives, we are called to wear multiple hats so that we can remain open to how God wants to use us. In our professional lives, we often find ourselves wearing many hats as well. I encourage you to lean on God for guidance rather than trying to handle this in your own strength. Position yourself to hear God's instruction because, ultimately, that new desire stirring within you may be what you are purposed for.

We are constantly evolving—we are not meant to stay the same; once I accepted that, it became easier to accept change. So, instead of becoming complacent out of fear, I decided to work on my ability to become flexible.

I began to think, I am allowed to be different from what I was a year ago or even yesterday. We should normalize that having thoughts like, 'I can't figure out what I want to do with the rest of my life,' or 'I want to switch my career,' are valid feelings that deserve compassion, not judgment. The moment I learned to stop being hard on myself, I gave myself the space to pursue my desires openly, understanding that these desires are birthed from my purpose. When you let go of what you perceive to be impossible, things may start to feel possible.

If you are not sure where to begin, first determine what you are good at and permit yourself to do it. Allow yourself to yield to what comes second nature to you, something that you can tell brings out the best in you and those around you. Do not be afraid to begin the journey of self-discovery—get to know who you are so you can fully embrace yourself, at any age. One of the greatest dangers in this world is believing we must conform to its ways, but we are called to live set apart, to stand out and be different. Your gifts and talents make a difference, and they are uniquely yours.

When we operate from a place of authenticity and allow others to see us in our vulnerability, it permits them to do the same. We are called to be the light in a dark place, and we get to reflect the character of Jesus on earth. I believe being a light and embracing our purpose is the new definition of success and is part of our calling as God's children.

4

The Journey of "I Do"

The example of marriage was one I received from my parents; they had been married for over 40 years. I was exposed to this love-filled covenant relationship my entire life, and I wanted one just like it. The dynamic between my parents was this: my dad called most of the shots, and my mom allowed him. My mom is gentle, but she is not one to express her emotions well, at least not in front of her children. Throughout their marriage, I saw submission at its finest. Culturally, this is what I witnessed: the men are dominant, and the women are subservient. In my mind, this was normal, so I attempted to mimic this while I was dating.

After I got married, I sacrificed myself to ensure my husband's sense of security. I submitted to the notion, "If you love me, then you will do what I ask," without realizing that I was losing myself in the process. My generosity and selflessness were taken for granted, and I lacked a backbone strong enough to have a healthy conversation about my expectations in marriage. Initially, I believed our relationship was founded on trust and open communication, but it did not remain that way. Our relationship did not have what I require my relationship to have now, Jesus at the center.

Watching my parents as a child, I came to idolize marriage and the idea of having a spouse. It was a beautiful phenomenon to witness, and I greatly admired my parents' union. It was something that I aspired to have in my lifetime, and so, when I met the man who was to become my husband, I felt like I hit the jackpot. Not once did I think about what a lifetime of marriage would entail, with all its intricacies. It is difficult to envision the tribulations in life when basking in the goodness of the moment. It was only after the losses of my closest family and after saying, "I do," that I realized I knew nothing about the work it would take to be married.

Reflecting on my journey, I've come to realize the significance of committing to someone who shares a deep devotion to God. Why? You might ask. You have probably heard the phrase, 'God is love.' Scripture reminds us that when someone is committed to God, it's much more likely that the relationship will reflect His values, making less room for things that go against Him. 1 Corinthians 13:4-7, KJV, depicts love as charity. The word charity is translated to "love" in other versions of the Bible, but in either case, this kind of love acts selflessly and seeks the good of others before oneself. Although I did not initially understand the concept of love as a sacrifice, I have come to realize that the term "sacrifice" is a powerful way to describe love in action.

The person you choose to spend your life with is one of the most important decisions you will make because it will impact the rest of your life. Know that the person who will make your life flourish will encourage change in you that allows for self-improvement and personal development; they will contribute to your growth.

It is essential to reflect on behaviors that contribute to consistent issues in your relationship. It is equally important to make changes to improve the quality of your relationship; these improvements will align with your growth. There is a difference between someone trying to change the core of you for their selfish reasons versus encouraging you to grow so you can feel empowered by your evolution.

I met my husband in 2012, and we officially started dating in September of that year. For simplicity, I'll refer to him as my husband throughout this section. My husband and I were quite inseparable. We were not just in love; we became best friends. One month after we became a couple, I experienced the loss of my aunt, Marie Lyvie Westerband (Tatie ViVi). She passed away in October of 2012, at fifty years old. My aunt was the epitome of kindness. I remember her sweet kisses and her compliments most; she was such a light. I distinctly recall a trip that my brother and I took with her and her church family, where I was incredibly inspired by her passion for Christ. Her love for Jesus is something that will remain with me. Although my husband explained that he had not been to a funeral before this, he would come to support me. This is where my extended family got to meet him for the first time.

We married in June of 2013, but it was not until years later that I realized I had given up so much of myself for the sake of keeping our marriage that I could barely recognize who I had become. I used to enjoy wearing make-up, hanging out with friends, and socializing with just about anyone I encountered in public. After we got married, I stopped wearing make-up, stopped going out as much, and limited male contacts to family members only; I was not allowed to have any friends of the opposite sex. I was told that I was not acting like a wife, and since I was now his wife, my actions needed to align.

Even though I knew I was trustworthy, his trust in me was a consistent battle. I did my best to display the love I could give, but the strains of mistrust tested our relationship, leading to countless arguments. Although this felt like love to me at the time, I later realized I could not express myself in this type of environment. I could not flourish—and that is not love.

Once you have built the confidence to stand by your beliefs and what you bring to your relationship, that is when you can lay down a healthy, solid foundation. Even with confidence, it will not magically make the wrong person right for you. It is important to be who you are, but it is equally important to grow into who you are becoming. We must determine when our partner might be holding us back. At times, this involves making the difficult decision to step away from someone you care about, even if that means being single for a while. Insecurities will break down a relationship, which is another reason why working on yourself before devoting yourself to someone is vital. If you are secure in yourself, it is harder for someone to change you into what they want you to become.

You see, at the end of the day, it is not our job to make other people feel secure in themselves. It is our job to model how secure we are in ourselves. Be an example and watch what that does to the people around you. This reminds me of Mahatma Gandhi's advice to 'be the change you wish to see in the world.' Living progressively tends to bring the right people into our path. When we operate at our best and embrace our light instead of dimming it, it naturally draws others to us and inspires them to strive for improvement. When you fully embrace your strengths and potential, this sets the stage to break down insecurities that can hinder your relationship. Therefore, we must commit to addressing our insecurities to foster successful relationships.

I was afraid to lose my husband, and as a result, I was willing to compromise myself to keep our relationship, a reminder that fear can sometimes cloud our judgment in love. Change is a natural part of any marriage because integrating another person into our lives necessitates adjustments; the key is to recognize when manipulation is taking place. Embracing change is essential, but it is equally important to ensure that these changes benefit the relationship. Once I began to compromise, more requests came, and it was like falling down a slippery slope. I slowly lost pieces of myself until I lost my sense of identity. He had molded me into what he saw fit for a wife, and I was so happy to be married that I did not notice.

The beginning of married life was going smoothly until the death of my sister. Three months after we said, "I do," while we were discovering each other as "newlyweds," my sister passed away that August. She was thirty-five years old with her whole life ahead of her. A beautiful soul and my very best friend. Sure, she annoyed me, yes, but she was also the reason I kept my zest for life! My sister had all the answers I did not, was sweet when I was salty, and kept me balanced.

My sister was a single mother of four kids who, at the time, were six, eight, eleven, and thirteen—three boys and one girl. After my sister passed away, my parents saw it fit to keep my sister's children together, so the kids moved into my parents' house, where my husband and I were living. Could you imagine the drastic difference in this household dynamic? We went from a household of four adults to a household of eight, with four of them being children. I don't know what kind of emotional struggles my husband experienced while adjusting, but I know I was a complete and total wreck after my sister died.

Losing my sister was the start of other losses to come. I wish my husband and I were equipped with the tools we needed to handle the losses that occurred in my family. We focused on individual ways to cope but neglected to learn marital coping strategies. I resorted to food as my comfort, so much so that it killed my sex drive. Nothing could bring me comfort the way a good ol' box of Snickerdoodles from Walmart could. I also lost so much of my sense of humor that I could barely take a joke. Not only had parts of my core changed, but the roles in our lives did as well, making our relationship suffer even further.

I played an active part in helping my parents raise the kids, and it was difficult for me. We were living in one house full of grieving people, and the last thing any grieving child wants is a new authority to answer to. Learning to cope with my grief moved me further from my role as his wife—I had other responsibilities I needed to focus on; duties that took priority over my husband.

My parents had lost their daughter, my niece and nephews had lost their mother, and I had lost my sweet, wild, and crazy "let's live in the moment" sister. She was such a big part of me, and I did not know it until she was gone. My husband and I accepted that the honeymoon period most couples enjoy was not part of our story. We grew to accept this and continued with the demands of life as they came. With little effort to mend the damage, the wedge between us grew. I assumed it would fix itself over time. I believed this level of grief was normal, that it would play its course, and eventually, we would get over it. Little did I know there was supposed to be an intentional effort to heal not just individually, but together. We failed to nurture healing within each other's lives.

I was struck by grief, going through the motions of each day. It took every ounce of strength I had to get out of bed, let alone go to work. Daily tasks became burdensome chores. In addition to this, I made it my responsibility to be present for my parents while they were grieving. I made it my duty to show up for the kids, to try to be a good wife, a loving sister, as well as a listening ear to how the death of my sister affected her friends and others in the community (because she was well-known and loved in the community).

As I wrestled with my own grief, supporting my husband became increasingly challenging. Once routine tasks, such as preparing dinner for him and maintaining our living space, became overwhelming. This went on for days, weeks, months, then years. A couple of years later, after my family started to find their footing in life without my sister, my brother died. In January of 2015, I received devastating news about my brother's passing. My brother battled a long road of illness through most of his life. He was diagnosed with lupus at the age of eighteen and was often in and out of the hospital. A team of specialists oversaw his care for more than twenty years. His body succumbed to cancer at the age of forty.

I would be remiss if I continued writing about him without acknowledging what a truly remarkable soul my oldest brother was. He was one of the sweetest people I've ever known. He lived his life in chronic pain yet still managed to put others' needs before his own. He was funny, kind, and welcoming to all, despite being constantly stared at, judged, and sometimes ridiculed. With lupus, the immune system attacks the body, causing damage to various organs. The kind of Lupus my brother had was both internal and external; it caused scaling and discoloration of the skin on his arms, chest, and face.

When we went out together, when anyone's eyes lingered a little too long, he would say, "It's okay, that's just how people are. They don't know." I appreciated his ability to empathize with others, despite the pain he had experienced himself, but it was not okay with me; most of the time, I would glare at them. Aspects of dealing with grief became compounded. I had to accept that I would never hear my siblings' voices again. They would not be a part of my kids' milestones, and the simple pleasures of having them in my life were gone in a moment. All I could do was try to pick up the pieces as my family was falling apart.

My husband admired my oldest brother for his kind heart and light presence, so when he passed away two years after we got married, it nearly crushed him, and our marriage suffered. I suggested therapy for my husband, but I did not accept the advice I was giving. It was years after my siblings died that I began receiving therapy, but the damage our marriage sustained felt irreparable. We did not just need individual therapy; we needed grief and marital counseling. I believe this would have fostered healing in our marriage. Without support, the problems between my husband and me continued to escalate. We were mentoring four young children who lost their only constant, their mother, because their fathers had little to no involvement.

My husband was a quiet guy when I met him, but his silence grew louder after grief hit. There was a level of indifference that he could not break free from, and this apathy led to ineffective communication. A barrier was built between him and me, and it reached a point where I could not penetrate it. It was this wedge that ultimately led to the decisions that tore our marriage apart. I resorted to doing what I do best, journaling and asking for God's help. Even though I was actively praying and seeking God for healing, I was angry with God for years. It was not until I became involved in a small group at my church in Florida that I began to study and apply the teachings of the Bible to my life.

God became the foundation of my healing, but I still sought solace in food, using it to fill some of the emptiness I felt inside. Although I did not struggle with binge eating as I had in my childhood and early adult years, overeating was something that made me feel full when I felt empty. Eating sweet treats masked itself as comfort when I really needed someone to hear my cries. This was a silent struggle that took years to overcome. I went back to implementing some of what I had learned from working at the eating disorder facility because, with grief being present and heavy, I lost my sense of self-control.

Growing up, my dad's sister, a strong matriarch in my father's family, gradually fell ill. Aunt Therese, whom we called "Manto", passed away, and again, I struggled deeply. A devout Catholic and fundamentally kind at heart, I could always count on her to brighten my day. Her sweet smile and strength offered me comfort. She had a quick-witted humor that would lighten even the heaviest moments. Her presence was a strong source of support and reassurance in my life, and her love for her family was unshakeable. Navigating losing her was tough. When I initially found out that her health was declining, I was in the process of healing from a corneal ulcer that caused permanent vision damage to my right eye. I was undergoing treatment for this, so my husband drove me to the hospital so that I could spend time with her before she died.

My maternal grandma was self-sufficient and lived alone about an hour away from us. My grandma started to experience an increase in falls and became afraid of living alone because of it. So, my mom encouraged her to move in with us. Our household then grew from a family of eight to a family of nine. As the matriarch on my mom's side, she was the glue that held our family together. My grandma's sense of humor and heart of gold filled our home.

My grandma, Marie Denise Westerband, we called "Grandma Chou Chou". was the reason my family became U.S. citizens in Rockland County, New York. My grandma long outlived my grandfather, who passed away in April of 2003. Although I don't remember much about my grandfather, I do recall receiving the best hugs from him. He gave me a nickname, "gwo patat," which translates from Haitian Creole to English as "big, sweet potato". I am certain he gave me this nickname because of my size, because I was a big girl then. Although I did not like it, I knew it was a term of endearment. I knew my grandpa was my grandma's rock.

Even after my grandpa died, she maintained her strength. Grandma Chou Chou taught me how to navigate complexities. She was patient, kind, and generous. An amazing woman, a wonderful cook, and a fantastic baker. She was full of wisdom. She encouraged me to be wise, loving, forgiving, and most importantly, assertive. I remember the sound advice she would give me about marriage. And honey, the topic of sex within the construct of marriage was no stranger to her!

One morning in July of 2015, I woke up to find an ambulance in front of our home. My dad called the paramedics because my grandmother wasn't feeling well. They took her to the nearest hospital, and that day, my grandma passed away. When I felt like life was getting better, someone else would pass away. With the losses we recently endured, my grandma's passing was one of the most difficult, but our family pulled together once again to support each other. At this point, we had developed a running joke that funerals had become our unofficial family reunions. I began to normalize death because it seemed to be happening far too often. During this time, I started to understand a few foundational truths and found myself growing stronger in my Christian faith.

As I continued to heal, I realized I could not let my pain consume me like it had before. My relationship with God helped me continue healing, but I had to ask God to teach me how to pour into the spaces in my life that I used to neglect due to grief, like my relationships, my personal goals, and self-care. I had to remind myself that healing needs to be intentional in every area. Healing is a lifelong commitment that helps us become who we are supposed to be.

5

Behind Closed Doors

Infidelity disrupted my life, presenting me with a decision of monumental difficulty. Should I stay and work through the heartache, or should I walk away? Although I stayed because I chose to forgive him, my actions proved otherwise.

In 2016, a year after our daughter was born, my husband and I began to make plans to move out of my parents' house. We moved out of my parents' home and into a lovely townhome that was minutes away. Although we were close, I felt guilty about leaving. I missed the kids, but I knew that I had to focus on my husband and my daughter more.

After being in our new home for a little over six months, I was doing laundry when I found a condom in my husband's pants pocket. I knew the condom did not belong to us because we were not using that method of protection. When I confronted him, he denied it was his. In my heart, I believed he would not lie to me because of his high expectations for honesty, but I was initially skeptical. Although I could not think of one, I knew there had to be an explanation for where the condom came from.

A few months later, I woke up to text messages chiming in on his phone in the middle of the night. I leaned over to check the messages and recognized that the number that came up was not saved in his contacts. The messages were sexually explicit, and immediately, my heart sank. I confronted him about the contents of the messages, but he explained that his friend pulled a prank on him with an unknown number, and I believed him.

After being accepted into nursing school, we decided to move back to my parents' house for support, as I would no longer be able to work full-time due to the demands of the nursing program. Thankfully, my parents were huge supporters of advancing education, so they were on board with the idea. It was while I was in nursing school, working to complete my RN degree, that I discovered explicit photos and messages pointing to another round of infidelity. Suddenly, it made sense why sex with my husband had changed. He was disengaged, and our intimacy took a toll. I thought I was doing something wrong. I believed I was the reason our physical connection faded, but after discovering the deceit, I realized that I was not the problem. I struggled to trust him again. It felt as though he had not only broken my trust but also disregarded my health and well-being.

When his infidelity came to light, I accepted I was not going to know all the details, but I was looking for some remorse, an apology, anything. I expected him to break down, cry, tell me something along the lines of, "I will never do this again." I thought he would plead with me not to leave him or tell me why he did it in the first place. I was anticipating hearing things I needed to change about myself, but to my surprise, none of that initially happened.

He denied it, and it was a battle to get him to talk to me about why he chose to cheat. Even though he did not beg me to stay, I still decided to stay.

He assured me that he had stopped cheating but I became obsessed with snooping through his phone and any other electronic devices linked to his accounts. I reviewed bank statements more closely to try to identify any unusual purchases. This spying became my new way of life, even though the essence of it drove me crazy. This went on for a month or two until I decided I could not do this anymore and tried to force separation.

I was going to take our daughter to stay at my sister-in-law's house so that I could get some much-needed space and time to clear my head, but he refused to let me leave. He took the keys to my car and said that if anyone was going to leave, it was him. We were living at my parents' house at the time, and he felt it was only right that I stay there with our daughter.

In my desperation, I decided to speak to his mom about what happened between us, because I felt she would get through to him in a way that I could not. I remember going to his parents' house for mediation, where they gave him a lecture on how he had better change before he loses his family.

Later, his mom came to our house to speak with us privately. She was mainly focused on me because she spent a large part of our conversation on forgiveness. Afterward, I decided to make a concerted effort to forgive him and start over. It hurt so badly that all I wanted to do was run, but I realized that I had to go through the pain if I wanted to come out on the other side of it.

I came up with the idea for us to write down our promises for a renewed relationship on paper, forgiving one another for the pain we caused each other during our marriage. He agreed to do this exercise with me, and afterward, we went to the beach and buried what we wrote in little glass jars in the sand. We had a moment that night that reassured me that things would turn out differently. Unfortunately, that was not the case. I continued to find evidence of affairs afterward, and I felt defeated in my attempts to act out the forgiveness I had agreed to. I decided to continue to forgive to save our marriage despite the continued affairs, hoping that things would change one day.

For months afterward, finding out about the first affair, I journaled heavily, which was my staple coping mechanism. I used positive affirmations daily in my journal entries, writing about the following: what our new future together would resemble, forgiving not just him but myself, speaking love into my life, and being grateful for the opportunity to start over with him. Doing this really helped me commit to my decision to stay.

I wanted our family to stay together. I knew that I did not want a divorce. I wanted us to raise our daughter in the same household. I knew that if I wanted our family to stay together, I would have to fight for it, but I was not sure where to begin. The last thing I wanted to do was raise our daughter in a single-parent household, but with the way our situation was unfolding, I felt defeated. Meanwhile, I prayed and asked God for the strength to do something I never thought I could do: forgive a husband who betrayed me.

Throughout this time, I began to feel inadequate, like I was not good enough for him and that we were not meant to be together. All I could think to myself was, *what is wrong with me?* My childhood feelings of inadequacy resurfaced, and I once again began to feel unaccepted. It took a lot of self-work for me to realize that I was not a victim, but that I had chosen to get involved with someone before I truly knew myself.

Before I accepted that our marriage was failing, the pain I experienced tore me down. I began to drink daily, smoke cigarettes, and act impulsively, and this lasted for roughly a year. Over time, I chose to allow my pain to build me up instead of tear me down. I decided to use the pain that I had experienced from the death of my family to the infidelity in my marriage to fuel my growth.

Although this was a process that took time and intentional efforts, it led me to challenge myself in areas I never thought I could. I began to focus on regaining my resilience. With this newfound empowerment, I hired a personal trainer, followed a workout routine, received a health and wellness coaching certification (a subject I am passionate about), and began writing this book.

6

Opting for Change

Less than a year after finding out about his affairs, my husband presented the idea of us moving from Florida to Georgia to start over. It would be a new beginning. We were moving to a place we had never heard of, and both our families thought the idea was irrational. I had just passed my nursing boards and was about to get a promotion to become an RN at my job, but I respectfully declined after my husband suggested we leave. Although my parents would never try to hold me back, I knew they needed help raising my niece and nephews. I also knew that moving out of my parents' house meant that the dynamic of our family would have to change yet again.

My parents were strained, mentally, emotionally, and financially. Grief continued to linger heavily in the air. They were giving all they had, but somehow it was not enough. Bills kept piling up, and emotional outbursts became common in our house. I knew something had to change. So, I rose to the occasion, searching for a solution to bring balance to our lives.

Since my parents assumed full guardianship of my sister's children, their role shifted from grandparent to parent, but compounded grief affected their ability to parent effectively. Although I anticipated that we would all make significant adjustments, I suggested that my brother and I take custody of the kids. My brother and I decided to divide custody of the children to provide them with closer attention. As a result, my parents would be able to settle into their retirement without the responsibility of raising my niece and nephews. Two of the children would reside with my husband and me in Georgia, while the other two would remain in Florida to move in with my brother. My oldest nephew was in his last year in high school and voiced that he did not want to switch schools during his senior year, so we reconsidered the need for him to relocate and decided to allow him to stay at my parents' house to graduate in Florida. After graduation, he would move in with my husband and me in Augusta, leaving my parents with an empty nest.

To minimize disruption to my youngest nephew's schooling, we drove up to get a head start on settling in. Once I discovered homeschools for our daughter and nephew and determined what I needed for my nephew's school transfer, I returned to Florida to pick him up. This was truly a trial-and-error process, and as we would find, nothing went as planned. Although the arrangement was mutually agreed upon among the adults, the kids were not thrilled about living apart. However, they came to understand the reasons why and made a sincere effort to adapt to the change.

Rather than staying with my brother like we arranged, my niece moved in with a friend and then returned to my parents' home shortly after. Meanwhile, my oldest nephew chose to continue living with my parents in Florida after graduating from high school. When my niece moved back home, she enjoyed being back in her homeschool, though she often struggled with following the rules. My nephew, on the other hand, liked attending school. He kept his mischief to himself and did his best to stay under the radar at home.

This change was to lighten the load on my parents, but during the process, I did not truly consider my husband's or the kids' perspectives. My husband was not expressive, and I did not explore his deepest thoughts on the matter at the time. Later, he revealed to me that, although he had agreed to the plan to take care of the kids, he envisioned a more traditional nuclear family.

Moving out of Florida felt like destiny—everything just seemed to fall into place with almost no effort. As we drove into Augusta, I remember freaking out. I had never seen so much greenery in my life. I was born and raised in Miami, so witnessing this scenery in person was shocking. I was a city girl about to get really acquainted with country living. The roads were curved and elevated, the commercial buildings resembled houses, and the people were distinctly different.

We began to settle into our new home, and my husband immediately started working. I started looking for a job and schools for the kids. I found a great daycare for our daughter, and I discovered which school my nephew was zoned for. Adjusting was challenging for us, especially for my nephew. He was away from his siblings, and we were in a small new town where we hardly knew anyone. However, after a few months, we began to settle in..

A year later, we moved to a new county in part for a better school district, which again meant new schools and more readjusting. Shortly after moving to a new county, I got a phone call from my mom. She explained that my niece was getting into the wrong crowd, and managing her behavior became exceedingly difficult. I brought this to my husband's attention, and we agreed to allow my niece to live with us in our two-bedroom apartment. We made room for my niece to move in with us. My parents flew in with her, and we worked on transitioning her to her new school. After we got her settled in, my parents flew back to Miami.

My husband and I drove my parents to the airport, a four-hour ride that marked the start of a new chapter in our lives. Even though it happened four years ago, I can remember it like it was yesterday. I tried to make the best of this situation that caught us both by surprise, but my efforts seemed to fail each time. I remember singing to my husband and dancing in the passenger seat as he drove us home from Hartsfield-Jackson Atlanta Airport, but he was disengaged. When we got home, he asked me if he could go out with some friends that night. I was confused because his asking for permission to go out was unusual. I responded, "Sure, why not?" But I was not prepared for what was about to happen next. After the airport ride, I settled back in at home, and he went out as he had asked to do. What I did not expect was that he would come home the next evening, after work. I immediately knew something was wrong, not physically wrong, but I sensed that he had made some poor choices the night he went out. I was hoping the choices he made would not be ones that would test our marriage, yet again.

When he finally decided to tell me the truth, which turned out to be exactly what I feared, he did so in tears, as if he knew this was not going to turn out well. His response brought yet another act of infidelity. I was grieved, and at that moment, it was I who chose to decide the fate of that night. I recalled a stranger who spoke with my husband and me outside the courthouse in Miami the day we got married. His advice was "never leave the house if you get into an argument." Disregarding that piece of advice, like I had done when I tried to force separation at my parents' house, I told him that night that he had to leave our home. When he asked to stay, I told him staying was no longer an option because he was not making "mistakes" but rather a series of bad decisions that affected our marriage. I again felt like my feelings, health, and safety were not his priority. While we were both in tears, he walked out the front door.

When I look back at it all, especially after we had later conversations about it, I realize that he was extremely overwhelmed and was unable to communicate this to me. He tried just as hard as I did to support my parents and our family, but that did not lessen the intensity of the changes we went through. He developed ways to cope with his emotions that, unfortunately, tested our marriage.

7

Facing Reality

After I asked my husband to leave, I found it incredibly difficult to adjust to his absence. Since I was the one who told him to go, I began to feel like I was the reason my family fell apart. It felt different knowing that I was the sole parent in the house. Managing school drop-offs and pick-ups, homework, and dinner on my own was painful, even though these were tasks I usually handled most nights when we were together. I did not consider the impact separation would have on us. The kids were missing him. When I asked him to leave, I was so consumed by grief that I based my decisions on my pain alone. Life felt different without him. I was lonely. I was weighed down by betrayal. I had to transition from sleeping next to my husband to no longer having him by my side, just one of the numerous adjustments I had not considered before asking him to leave. During our separation, I purchased a weighted blanket so that I would not feel so alone; it brought me comfort and a sense of protection without him nearby.

During our separation, he told me he was staying at a friend's house. He would call every day to ask if I was ready for him to come home, but the pain I felt would not allow me to admit that I wanted him to return. After we had been separated for weeks, he shared that the friend's house he was staying at was the woman he had an affair with. I made it clear to him that if he wanted to reconcile, he needed to inform her of his commitment to our family and that he would no longer entertain the situation they created. I suggested she come to our house so he could break things off with her directly. When she arrived at our home, I walked outside to speak with her. I briefly told her that she would not like what she was about to hear, but she needed to hear it from him. I went back inside while they conversed, thinking that he was ending their relationship once and for all; however, interactions with her grew more frequent afterward. I knew then that their relationship had not ended.

A few days later, he began spending nights at her place. He would pack his gym bag at night and tell me he was going to stay with her and that he would be back later. After weeks of this, I could no longer handle it. I told him he had to decide—and he did. He chose to stay home. I sought guidance and prayed to figure out how to get through this season of betrayal. When he decided to return home for good, I agreed to help him get his belongings from her house. I helped him pack what he left at her place, and we drove back home. I thought his return meant that he would be home for good, but after days of being home, I noticed he was uncomfortable. He was unsettled, frustrated, heartbroken even. It was as if he could not see the family he had slipping through his fingers. It became evident that he was not the same person I had married.

One evening, as we sat down to eat, I noticed he was not truly present during dinner. Instead of engaging in conversation with me and the kids, he was quiet, drinking alcohol, and playing sappy music. I was hopeless and told him that if he did not want to be at home with us anymore, he did not have to stay. Shortly after, my husband packed his belongings and left our house. His decision to leave broke my heart again. Even though one of my worst fears had become a reality, my love for him did not fade. On numerous occasions, he went through moments of regret and would call, asking to return home, but I could not overcome the betrayal. He apologized for causing damage to our relationship, but I could not open myself up to the possibility of getting hurt by him again. I was trying to keep myself together. I knew I had a family to support, so allowing his infidelity to take me down, I knew, was not an option. I started attending a local church, and I ran to God like I had never done before. If I had not, I do not know where I would be today. I created a prayer closet, wrote prayers on flashcards, and prayed for him. I prayed for us individually and for our marriage to be restored. I also prayed for our families.

I was leaning on what I knew would help me feel better. Journaling was one of those coping skills that helped me put things into perspective. I journaled more than I had ever journaled in my life. It became a multiple-time-a-day coping mechanism that I know helped me navigate my situation. I also wrote poems to help me release the pain.

At the time of our separation and for a while after, I was unemployed, living off savings and COVID stimulus checks. God provided every step of the way, and my family and I never lacked. During my period of unemployment, I was given the space I needed, which was crucial to my healing. When the kids were at school, I had the house to myself. My home became my sanctuary, a place I could fall apart and ask God to put me back together. We had a large sectional that could be taken apart, and I moved a piece of it into the kitchen by my plastic table, creating a little corner where I could read, write, scream, and cry comfortably. The sunlight was the brightest in that room. I enjoyed the warmth on my skin from the sun coming through the small window. I would make my way to the living room to praise and worship aloud. I would sing and shout to the top of my lungs, and, boy, did it bring me a sense of relief.

During our separation, I hired a Christian life coach who kept me strong and held me accountable for my actions. Her goal for my husband and me was reconciliation, with an attempt to refer him to her husband for coaching sessions. There were many times I wanted him to return home, but I knew from my experience with him that the outcome may not work out if I gave in. My new request to him was simple: if he wanted to start over, he had to end his current relationship, move out on his own, and seek counseling. I thought it was tough to require this of him, but my life coach assured me I was on the right track. Having someone who provides sound advice rooted in biblical principles was important because it gave me the validation and encouragement I needed to make decisions with clarity and confidence

My coach explained that it was necessary to hold higher standards for myself and that if my husband truly wanted things to work out, he would put in the effort to make it happen. I stayed consistent with all my healing modalities—I listened to teachers who helped me stay focused, like Pastor Jerry Flowers, Dr. Dharius Daniels, Tony Gaskins, and Pastor RC Blakes. They played on my

YouTube channel almost every day. I took notes and read books that would help me through this process. This was alongside attending church, participating in a small group, and staying connected to the Word of God through the Holy Bible. I did whatever I could to help heal my soul. I waited for my husband to make changes in his life that I needed to see before he could come back, but unfortunately, that time never came. After my husband and I remained separated for about six months, I decided to file for divorce. I relied on my friends and family to keep me strong, and I drew on everything I had learned along the way to guide my healing, because I could not do it alone.

8

From Pain to Power

My dad had multiple chronic conditions but he took care of our family well despite his ailments. He was the kind of man who went above and beyond. When you asked him to do something, he would go the extra mile. He loved to see people happy. I found out that my dad's condition started to worsen after he sustained a fall that put him in the hospital. Subsequently, he often fell, experienced gastrointestinal bleeds, and suffered multiple strokes.

About a year after my separation, my parents shared with me that they wanted to move to Augusta. My dad's condition made relocating him across the state something we had to plan intricately because as his sickness progressed he became immobile. Since my dad was in and out of nursing homes and hospitals, we carefully strategized how we would move him safely. The COVID-19 pandemic swept the nation, creating new healthcare guidelines that affected visitation in healthcare facilities. My mom was going through a difficult season because of this change. She could not stay overnight with my dad at the nursing home, nor was she allowed to be with him when he was admitted to the hospital. Since my parents were between houses during his health decline, a close friend of the family offered my mom to stay at her place while my dad stayed in the nursing home.

My dad was discharged from the nursing home in January of 2021, and my brother graciously invited our parents to live with him in his apartment as we prepared for their move to Augusta. I had been working with my parents to secure an apartment so they could move right in. We were finally able to strategize a plan to get my dad to Augusta. My brother and middle nephew rented a van, positioning my dad as comfortably as possible, and drove the nine-hour ride with my parents. My dad's health did not improve after the move. He had frequent doctor's appointments that required medical transport. Doctor's appointments turned into hospital admissions. The last two weeks of my dad's life were spent in hospice care at home with 24-hour nursing care provided by an agency. My mom and I took on the responsibility of caring for my dad in addition to the home health support because the visiting nurse would come as needed; however, his medications required administration around the clock.

Witnessing my dad's condition worsen was the most difficult part about caring for him. He was no longer the same person; he had lost a significant amount of weight, and he barely spoke. My heart shattered watching him deteriorate before my eyes. My mom was anchored and cared for him like a soldier, but I can only imagine what my mom experienced during his decline. At the end of a long day caring for him, I was able to go home, but my mom, on the other hand, remained by his side.

While my dad was in hospice care, I took a leave of absence from work to help my mom take care of him. My Dad was a stubborn man, so he was not going down without a fight. My parents were lovebirds. They were the kind of older married couple that would dance in the middle of the kitchen for no reason and lock arms around each other as they made a toast during a celebration. In my heart, I could only think that he was holding on because he did not want to leave her behind.

On the day my brother flew in to see my dad, he walked into the room where my dad was and shut the door behind him. When he came out, he told us that he had prayed the Prayer of Salvation with my dad and assured him that he would take care of our family. Shortly after this, I went to the grocery store to get food to make dinner when I received a call that my dad had died.

A different version of me was born after his death. I became unapologetically more myself than ever before. It felt as though he left a part of himself behind to help me make it through life—because if anyone understood how challenging life could be, it was him.

We arranged for his funeral to take place back home in Miami. I created his eulogy and read it at his funeral. My friends flew in and drove in from all over to support me that day, an act of service I will cherish for life. This moment marked another pivotal time in my life. It proved to me that I could display a strength I did not know I had. There are no words to describe the feeling we get when we hear news that a loved one has passed. The losses I have experienced felt like I had lost a piece of myself when they left. When I read my dad's eulogy in front of his casket, I left my sunglasses on and allowed my tears to flow down my face the entire reading. We placed white roses on his casket and said our final good-byes as they lowered him into the ground. God kept me together, even when I felt like I was falling apart.

When my family and I got back to Augusta, his loss started to settle in. His absence felt more real to me. A couple of things that helped me cope with losing him were keeping the last blanket he used. I kept it as it was for 2 months before I washed it. I felt that if I kept it as it was, I would still have some of him here with me. Also, when I was alone, I found myself still talking to him because I could not get used to the idea of never sharing a moment of laughter or hearing his voice again.

Our family dynamic changed after my dad was gone. We transitioned from having a leader to me feeling like I had to become one. I knew at that point I would really have to put on my "big girl pants" and make things happen. To begin with, I knew I had to move my mom out of their apartment because he passed away in their bedroom. It was time to make some serious life choices. The death of my father lit a fire inside of me. I was learning to take the world by storm, recognizing more now that our tomorrow is not promised. I bought my first home, inviting my family to move in. This closely resembled our living arrangements in Florida. My household went from a family of 4 to a family of 7, and a dog. I completed my health and wellness coaching certification and opened an LLC in my name. It is in moments like these that I'm reminded that my parents equipped me and that God placed a part of Himself within me so I could thrive.

9

Finding Resilience

I began to accept that my life was not going to happen the way I expected. Things were falling apart quicker than I could try to put them back together. Instead of fighting it, I began to relinquish some of this perceived control and let God be the driver. These twists and turns that kept taking me by surprise brought me to a point where I had to ask God, *what are these lessons supposed to be teaching me*?

During my separation from my husband, I found out that I was pregnant with our second child. When I revealed the news, he seemed utterly surprised. He did not think the second child was his, but I quickly explained that he was the last person I had been intimate with and that he was absolutely the father. During our separation while we were still married, I initiated intimacy with him in hopes that I would reignite the connection we once shared. I thought that if he could remember our bond, maybe it would convince him to return home. It was a moment of pure desperation, and afterward, I could not believe I put myself in the position of being 'the other woman.'

Disappointed in myself, I struggled to come to terms with the reality that he had already moved on. I asked God to help me accept that bringing this baby into the world would look different than what I wanted. Being a single parent reminded me of my sister's life. After she got married, my sister and her husband moved to Texas with my oldest nephew and niece, who were babies at the time. Unfortunately, things did not work out between her and her husband. My dad came to her rescue, purchasing plane tickets for her and the kids to fly home.

Although returning home gave her a fresh start and the support of family, I watched my sister navigate single motherhood—and it looked incredibly hard. I admired the strength of my sister and how she was able to create something out of nothing to support her family but the idea of being a single mom crushed me. I remember visiting my sister's house in my early twenties. I would watch her feed her family of five on a budget. She would come from work with toilet tissue and bags of food from the job. Her dinner menu items consisted of dishes like beanies and weenies with white rice, fried bologna with sauteed onions, and boxed mashed potatoes and cubed ham in gravy, to name a few. I frequented her house, and we would spend hours talking. She would share her life experiences with me, and even with nothing but admiration for her, I knew it was a life I did not want.

I thought that because I took all the right steps, getting married before having my first child and accomplishing goals before marriage, that my outcome would be different; however, I was wrong, and it truly became a humbling experience. When my ex-husband and I did not work out, all I wanted to do was run home. However, since I did not want to make a rash decision to pack up and move back home without being certain that was the right move, I took frequent trips back home instead.

Going home felt peaceful. Every few months, I would pack, load the car, and drive home with the kids and our dog, Luca. This drive typically takes about 8 hours, but with all the needs of the passengers, a trip home would easily turn into a twelve- or thirteen-hour ride. However, the extra time did not deter me from taking frequent trips. I was unemployed with three dependents and an unborn baby in a state where I had no family and barely any friends, so even with the trips, I constantly contemplated moving back home during this time. I prayed and sought God for guidance on what to do next. After a few months, the decision became clear. I remember lying in bed in my old room when I felt in my spirit, "Something is here for you, don't move back home. If you do, you'll miss it." I conjured the guts to listen and stayed put.

I returned after that trip knowing that I had to settle in Augusta. I began looking for a job because my savings were almost depleted, and I had no other means to support my family. Journaling remained a powerful coping skill for me, and I was in my prayer closet daily with index cards and the Holy Bible. I prayed for our baby, myself, our daughter, my ex-husband, and our families. Over time, God started to shift my mindset from one of weakness and defeat to one of strength and victory.

From the moment I discovered I was pregnant, I made it a point to talk to our little one every day, cherishing every chance to build a bond before they entered the world. I began dreaming up names, imagining their laugh, their smile, and pouring all the love in my heart into this tiny life growing inside me. I knew I had to stay strong, not just for myself, but for our baby. I also understood that this journey further into motherhood would demand more courage, patience, and resilience as our children grew.

I tried to look at every possible positive I could in my situation without focusing on the trauma I was going through. I had to get used to the idea that my children would not have their father physically present in their daily lives. I decided to counteract the negative feelings with positive affirmations, writing a new list of what I wanted for my life and my family. I wanted the kids to be healthy, I wanted to be able to provide for them, and I wanted their father to be an active participant in his children's lives. I prayed over it as the days went by.

One morning, I woke up to take the kids to school, I was in my first trimester of pregnancy. The kids hopped in the car and I began to open my car door to get in. When I opened the door, I felt a light pop in my lower abdomen and felt fluid flow down my leg. I told the kids to sit tight, that I had to use the bathroom, and immediately rushed back inside the house. When I reached the bathroom, I saw exactly what I was afraid to see: blood. I quickly cleaned up, added layers of protection to my undergarment, and went back outside to take the kids to school.

I immediately drove to the emergency room after the kids went to school. On the way to the hospital, I called my ex-husband and explained to him what had happened. I asked him to meet me at the emergency room for support. I also called my parents to let them know what was happening, but they became so worried that it felt like I had to comfort them during my time of need. When my ex-husband arrived, he was also not of much comfort. As his usual new self, he was present but distant. He was concerned but seemed detached. The emergency room physician informed us that what I was experiencing was more than likely a miscarriage, but for confirmation, I had to follow up with my OB-GYN. My doctor suggested a blood test called Beta HCG to check for a hormone produced only during pregnancy, to determine if the levels were normal. I had to go back to the office every few days to see if the levels were decreasing, which would confirm the miscarriage.

When I went back to my OB-GYN for my third follow-up, the results of the Beta HCG were lower than my last two visits, which meant that there was no longer a viable pregnancy. The HCG levels continued to drop with every subsequent visit. After the miscarriage was confirmed, my doctor had me continue coming in for tests to ensure I would not need a procedure called a Dilation and Curettage (D&C), which removes tissue from the lining of the uterus and any remaining fetal tissue. Thankfully, I did not need to undergo this procedure because my body expelled the baby on its own. Another nightmare came true—I miscarried our baby.

It was a slow process to recover. I was in pain for weeks, not just physical pain, but I was emotionally wrecked. Yet again, I felt defeated. I thought to myself, *Why is this happening to me? Why do I keep losing everything?* The day of the miscarriage, my ex-husband followed me home after we left the hospital. While the kids were still in school, he stayed with me as I struggled to process what had happened. I could sense that he felt sorry for me because even after everything we went through, he once again suggested that maybe he should come back home, but I was not looking for him to return out of pity. I knew I had not touched the tip of the iceberg with healing, and losing our baby was going to compound my grief further. So, after he picked up the kids from school and brought them to my house, he went home.

I had to adapt to my new reality after losing the baby. I had to reset my expectations and come to terms with the fact that the plans I believed God had for me were different from what I had envisioned, once again. You can imagine the struggle I faced in coping with this fresh loss. Throughout my pregnancy, I pushed myself to take care of my body, determined not to lose this baby, but despite my efforts, I still experienced a heartbreaking loss. While trying to remain strong during my separation from my ex-husband while single-parenting, I could not help but wonder if the baby absorbed so much of my strife that it became too much for him or her to handle. I felt like I had failed. I was riddled with thoughts of guilt. I asked myself, what could I have done to prevent this from happening?

My responsibilities did not stop because of what was happening, so I had to continue addressing the demands of life. My niece, who was a senior in high school at the time, stepped in to help me manage daily tasks. My emotions were unstable, and I was in a lot of pain. Managing my household alone was nearly impossible. It was difficult for her to step up in this role because she fostered such excitement for the arrival of the new baby, but she found a routine that helped me and worked as hard as she could to stick with it. Though she had behavioral struggles in the past, she quickly showed growth and a willingness to help. She had driven before, but let me tell you, she became proficient in her driving skills during this time because of how much I depended on her to drive while I recovered. I hated showing my vulnerability, but her unconditional support reminded me it was okay to lean on someone during my time of need.

While I felt like all this was happening to me alone, I had to remember that my nephew, who was fourteen at the time, and my six-year-old daughter also had to process a loss. I believe they deserved to know what happened. Since they had been there every step of the way, I explained to them that I had lost the baby, I wanted to show them that it was okay to lose something or someone you expected to have, and that letting go of unmet expectations is necessary to move forward in life.

My life is a testament to the truth that everything we face serves a greater purpose, and what God has prepared for us is far greater than anything we could design ourselves. Things may not work out exactly how you expect them to, but that does not mean that you should stop believing that good things are meant for you.

My family saw me go through grief in many ways. The way they see me handling losses will, to some degree, affect the way they handle theirs. I knew that what I showed them mattered. Months after the miscarriage, my ex-husband presented me with a heartfelt apology for everything we had gone through. It was hard to forgive him because I felt like he bailed on me and our family, but I knew that this was going to be the start of where the real work on mending and co-parenting would begin.

I was so focused on my own pain during that season of life that I could not see how our divorce was affecting the rest of our families. I also did not consider his struggles as much as I did my own. Through this, I learned that showing empathy toward someone who caused me pain allows me to see the circumstance from a perspective beyond my own.

In hindsight, I realize that my identity had been shaped by the roles I played, and somewhere along the way, I lost sight of who I was. When our marriage fell apart, I recognized that the level of importance I placed on those titles had become a form of idolatry. I had to ask God for forgiveness and strength to let go. One thing that has helped me significantly through healing from our failed marriage is deciding not to take what happened in our relationship personally. As a result, I have been able to forgive him. We stepped into more effective co-parenting of our beautiful daughter without lingering tension. I became determined to build a new kind of relationship with him—one rooted in mutual respect and healthy communication.

10

The Return

A year after my father died, my ex-husband asked to return home, even though he was still living with the woman with whom he had had an affair. In my moment of complete vulnerability, I agreed. I was afraid, though. I thought to myself, *what would my family think? What would my friends think?* I wanted my family back together again, so I decided that their opinions about my decision did not matter.

Before he returned home, I gathered my mom, nephews, and daughter, sat them down in the family room, and announced that my ex-husband would be returning home. I was not sure how they would respond, but I explained that it was important to me for our family to be together. Even after explaining this, they all looked confused. I could tell no one understood why I had chosen this route; however, I did not let that determine my decision. Although I stood by my decision, when he showed up at the house, I had every intention of demonstrating that I meant business. Although I allowed him to return, I was not going to be taken advantage of again. I told him that he could not sleep in the same room as me, his clothes had to remain in the car, and that he had to earn my trust back. There were stipulations for how things were going to go, and he did not like it.

Although I decided he could return, I could not make it easy for him. I was not ready to accept the hard work that came with my decision. Deciding to let him come back was tough, especially considering he did not fulfill my initial request to leave his girlfriend's house and focus on his own healing before attempting to reconcile. As he insisted on returning without making those changes, I eventually yielded and allowed him back in. I felt like I was already generous by giving him another chance, so I wondered, what more did he expect from me? This was a lot to handle! I asked him, bluntly, "What do you want from me?" He explained that he wanted things to return to normal, for me to embrace him with open arms, show him love and affection, and allow him to sleep next to me. Quite frankly, I did not know how to give him what he needed to make him feel better. I was worried about my own mental and emotional well-being and the amount of effort it took for another chance in the first place.

As I reflect, I realized that my blunt approach was not what he expected. While it was important for him to understand my expectations, I now see that I could have approached his return with more empathy and sensitivity. His desire for things to return to normal, to feel loved and embraced, and to share the same bed was a clear expression of his need for reassurance and connection. Unfortunately, coming from a broken place, I was unable to provide that.

Later that day, he told me that he would have to go back to his girlfriend's house because she had left her work gear in his car. To me, his desire to go back to "return her things" was his uncertainty regarding wanting to remain home with his family, so I told him that if he wanted to stay, and if this was the decision he was making, he could not look back. He had a look on his face that screamed he was bothered by my inability to bend at his request. After staying at my house for less than twenty-four hours, he told me that he had to leave and asked me not to hate him. A few weeks later, he called to tell me that he was going to propose to her and told me not to wait for him. They later married, and I had to learn how to live with their decision peacefully. Although my family was disappointed with the outcome, they remained extremely supportive of me during this time.

His quick decision to get married caught me off guard, but I was determined not to let it defeat me. I continued on my healing journey and arrived at a place where I started to pray for acceptance for what had come. I asked God to grace me with love, perseverance, and the ability to show my daughter how to handle a situation like this with dignity. I wanted her to be able to enjoy getting to know her future stepmom, and I did not want their relationship to be affected by the situation between her dad and me. A lot of how I handled his relationship with her was for our daughter's sake. I explained to my ex-husband that I would respect his new wife. As a former wife, I recognize the significance of respecting the unity of marriage. I also made it clear that she would be considered an extension of my family because of the role she would play in our daughter's life as her stepmom. After experiencing this news, I now faced questions with myself—how would I deal with this new chapter in my life? How could I show our daughter, my niece, and my nephews that no matter what I went through, I was still going to show up for myself and them? How would I show them that even through trials and tribulations, you can persevere? I went through a range of emotions in such a short amount of time, and I had to allow myself to feel them. I knew there would be more to life after this.

Since our daughter was going to have a new stepmom, I knew forgiving him alone was not going to be enough in this relational dynamic. I would also have to learn how to be inclusive while pushing past my anger, pain, and betrayal. I had to figure out how I was going to include our daughter's stepmom in her life without being bitter about my marriage ending. I prayed, fasted, and asked God to give me the strength that I knew I could not find on my own. God helped me realize that the first gesture I could make was opening a line of communication with her stepmom, as the relationship between her and our daughter would grow closer as the years progressed.

A few months after they got married, I asked if his wife and I could exchange numbers with the agreement to get in touch when needed. I can see how this situation would be hard for many to perceive, but you must remember that taking steps toward healing means not holding on tightly to the things that have caused you pain. When I shifted my mindset from victim to victor, my feelings toward life also shifted. I started to look at every possible scenario as an opportunity to learn and share how I navigate through traumatic experiences. Every day is not a walk in the park, but since I strive to get the most out of life, it inspires me daily to welcome growth, change, and continuous improvement.

I was able to accomplish things I never thought possible after I invested in myself. I allowed my ex-husband and his wife to visit our daughter at my house and permitted sleepovers at her dad's house so she could continue living the fullest version of her own life in this new season. Our daughter did not have a say in what happened between her father and me, so I did not want her to suffer at the hands of what once broke me. I learned how to navigate birthdays, holidays, and the ups and downs of our blended family. Through it all, I remained cordial and accommodating for the sake of our daughter's happiness and my own healing. I chose to set aside the pain of what I had experienced with him. Instead, I focused on modeling Christ-like behavior. In choosing love, I discovered the strength to offer genuine forgiveness.

Over time, it became easier to prioritize my well-being. You must keep at the forefront of your mind that the health and wellness of you and your family are more important than any circumstance. When you decide to forgive someone, you are refusing to let the pain they caused dictate your actions. If reconciliation is what you choose, do it with God in the center and with a support system behind you. Take the time you need to heal and know that it's okay to ask for help when you need it.

Each time things changed between us, I had to go through Kübler-Ross' 5 Stages of Grief all over again: denial, anger, bargaining, depression, and acceptance, which was absolutely exhausting. Looking back, the exhaustion and pain made me vulnerable, and I made many decisions out of emotion, which was not the best way to handle the trials that came our way.

I implore you not to make decisions based on pure emotions. Remaining in the pain cycle will have us stuck living in the past, which will affect the people around us. Our minds are so powerful, and the emotions we are feeling create a chemical response in our body, so our bodies do not always know the difference between reality and make-believe. This means that when we dwell in the past, our minds are reliving our experiences, which forces our bodies to go through the trauma all over again. This keeps people in a perpetual state of misery without realizing that our repeated thoughts are causing us to remain stagnant. Living in your painful history can damage your present and future, but learning from your history will allow you to create the life and relationships you desire.

11

Rising to the Occasion

After my father passed away, I stepped into a full-time caretaker role for my two nephews. They were fifteen and sixteen at the time. My family had endured many losses by then, and I could sense my mom's exhaustion from the grief. My dad's passing was the final straw for her. Assuming responsibility for my nephews would test my resilience, but it would also give my mom a chance to rest. This endeavor would require me to commit myself to raising them full-time, but I was confident in my ability to rise to the occasion.

Living with teenagers and a school-aged child is like living life underneath a microscope. With the kids watching every move, it gave ample opportunities for self-reflection. I became more aware of my interactions with them, paying closer attention to how my behavior affected the kids'. I took responsibility for my mistakes, owning my flaws. Raising the kids with a more humanistic approach fostered healthy relationships with them, ones that were open and transparent. I did not shy away from apologizing for actions that may have hurt them, exemplifying the importance of humility. The kids helped me recognize that explaining myself to them does not mean that they are overprivileged. The mindset I developed as a parent evolved from my early twenties, when I helped my parents raise my sister's children. Over time, my approach shifted from a strict parenting style to one that allowed my children to feel seen and heard. My heart broke for my niece and nephews, and I was stressing myself and them out to show them that I cared. I later realized, though, that after my sister died, the kids probably just needed me to be their aunt, not their mom.

Back then, I set out to operate under the following authoritarian models, like my dad. One of my favorite models was "Do it, because I said so". The kids quickly taught me that living by this model would not get me far. We faced many challenges in the household while I was learning how to transition from a fun aunt to a mother figure. Now that I have adjusted my expectations and am clearer about what I desire to teach my children, our relationships look different than the ones I had with my parents growing up. They talk to me openly and trust me with their feelings, and I make it a point to really listen. My insight into different parts of their lives matters, even though they may not always choose to take my advice.

It's crucial that my children can confide in me. A home that prioritizes fostering healthy relationships sets the stage for cultivating healthy relationships in life. Promoting environments where difficult conversations can be had strengthens and deepens relationships. After all, effective communication serves as the cornerstone for developing proper coping mechanisms and ultimately leads to successful outcomes.

Fulfilling a child's needs is necessary, but addressing their wants is life-changing for them. Showing them that you care about more than just the basics—a roof over their head and food on the table—builds a stronger connection and deepens their level of trust. Before I took the time to reevaluate my role as a parent, I was overly critical of them. I would wait for any opportunity to provide corrections, watching their words and actions closely. I mostly pointed out where they needed improvement, paying little attention to acknowledging their wins.

Over time, I realized the importance of recognizing their progress. Affirming them helped us build a stronger bond and promote positive behaviors. Celebrating their accomplishments not only encouraged them but also built a deeper level of respect and appreciation in our relationship. Life is hectic and sometimes feels like my family could be the plot of a sitcom, but every experience has been a lesson in becoming a better person. The challenges have contributed to my growth. The lessons I learned and the mistakes I made molded me into the person I am now. By fostering transparency and honesty with my children, our bond has become stronger. Through demonstrating humility and perseverance and modeling self-reflection, I believe I've shown them that they, too, can overcome challenges.

12

Navigating Transitions

About two years after I miscarried, my daughter returned from a family vacation that included her dad and his wife and announced, "Mommy, I am going to have a sibling." Upon hearing this, my heart sank. Not only was this an addition to our family, but this was also something I was not prepared to navigate. I was afraid that my daughter would be forgotten after the baby was born, that she would develop a sense of resentment regarding having a new baby in the family.

When my ex-husband and I were raising our daughter, he was not as engaged in fatherhood as I had hoped. These past experiences contributed to my feelings of uncertainty about the new baby. While my initial reaction was not one of excitement, I knew I had to work on accepting this new family dynamic for the sake of my daughter. I prayed that her stepmom would give birth to a healthy baby and that they would foster a good home for him. Though I had filled my thoughts with optimism, when the baby arrived, I unexpectedly grieved. Even though I coped well with the news of our blended family growing, the baby's arrival stirred my emotions. I realized a large part of my grief stemmed from my miscarriage, which resurfaced painful memories. This revealed to me that I had to work through my emotions in therapy.

My daughter's eighth birthday rolled around, and she made it clear that her baby brother had to be invited to the party. Watching my ex-husband care for their baby during the party reminded me of the lack of effort he put into caring for our daughter when she was a baby. I checked my thoughts and countered the negative thinking by finding solace in recognizing that he had evolved as a person. People change, and I accepted that this was part of his growth. I embraced that his wife and the baby get to experience this improved version of him, which is a blessing for them.

We took tons of pictures throughout the party. My daughter had a blast, and the girls seemed to have enjoyed themselves. As we were cleaning up, I realized I had not taken any pictures of my daughter with her new baby brother. This moment was important for me to give her, one that solidified that I could put aside my emotions to provide a better experience for my daughter. The baby was already snug in the carriage, and they were ready to go, but I asked them if I could take a family picture of the four of them. I was grateful when they agreed, allowing me to capture this beautiful moment.

Leaving the celebration, I felt a sense of accomplishment. Although awkward, it was a blessing to bring our families together to celebrate our daughter. Once again, by the grace of God, I showed up—genuine, in maturity, and with love. If there's one thing to take away from my story, it's this: focus on the bigger picture. Look beyond the challenges and concentrate on the moments that can bring your family joy. Special occasions can be difficult when family dynamics change, but they are once-in-a-lifetime opportunities to create memories with your loved ones. God gave us the ability to make celebrations. While planning for them, it is vital to understand that our emotions will shape the atmosphere. Your mood can significantly impact the outcome of an event.

I encourage you to take time to work on yourself before the coming together of your blended family, whether that's writing out your feelings to process them, talking to a confidant, praying about it, or finding a healthy way to alleviate any concerns that come up for you. Be mindful of your emotional state and acknowledge your current situation. If you suppress emotions, it may show up in a way you did not intend.

When we mask our struggles, it can keep us in denial. This can prevent us from realizing that we need to make a change. Take the time to ask yourself, can I begin the restorative work without accepting that there's something I need to work on? If we don't acknowledge where we are, we will not have a starting point to work from; as a result, neither you nor the people around you will reap the benefits of your healing.

13

A Turn Toward

Happily, Ever After…

Healing became my top priority after my husband and I separated. I knew I had to address what was broken within me before I could move forward. That separation drew me closer to God, and I began to deepen my relationship with Him after we parted ways. After the deaths of my maternal aunt and siblings, I busied myself with dedicating much of my personal time to taking care of my family's needs, which led me to burn out. After my divorce, I dedicated more time to myself. I meditated daily, increased self-care practices, and hired a personal trainer. I reinvented my social life, spending more time with friends and dating. I revitalized my thinking. I used a life coach to help keep me accountable and committed to attending therapy regularly.

Repeating old mistakes was something I could no longer afford. I was genuinely tired of heartache, so I needed to do something different to get different results. This meant I had to work on myself before I could commit to anyone else. I had to make better decisions, not just for me but also for my family. There is a lot of pressure in being the sole provider of the household. In this role, the decisions I make have a greater impact on my family, so I can no longer repeat the same mistakes.

Through the years of navigating grief, it was essential to make room for my personal life. One way I was able to take my mind off my responsibilities was through my social life. I would go out with friends, take vacations, and plan self-care days with my girlfriends. Dating was casual, but it became rather serious as I craved commitment. I tried to be intentional about who I allowed in my life, but this was confusing as I re-entered the dating scene. I knew I wanted a God-fearing man—someone who desired to be a loving father, a devoted husband, and a positive role model. With that in mind, I approached dating carefully until I found a man I believed was truly worthy of commitment. Amid my healing journey and while keeping these priorities at the forefront of my mind, I found someone who I knew could be the man I was looking for. He was assertive and knew what he wanted out of life. He was persistent in his approach, and I loved it. I had finally found the new love I was praying for. We became official quickly. It was as if he knew exactly how to provide the love I needed, one that nourished my soul, but after some time, I realized that there were aspects of our relationship that required further attention. If we continued down the path of misunderstandings and arguments, our relationship would be doomed to fail. Even though we managed to resolve our differences each time, these conflicts made me feel unsettled in our relationship. I was missing a sense of peace about being with him.

Poor communication affected our relationship, and my struggles to express my needs were rooted in the pain of my failed marriage. I knew that unresolved communication could slowly erode what we had, yet I endured it, hoping things would change. Our approaches to conflict were fundamentally different, which only made resolution more challenging. He was confrontational, and I avoided issues; he had no filter, and I would sugarcoat my concerns. Bridging this gap required serious effort. Not only did we have very different communication and conflict resolution styles, but we also had busy schedules.

In this new season, I prioritized myself, so making time for him was challenging, and his constant work travel also made it difficult to spend time together. After about six months of trying to create a healthier relationship dynamic, we decided to end the relationship, agreeing to remain friends.

While I was newly single, a friend introduced me to someone new. He was handsome, funny, and edgy. I enjoyed getting to know him and was looking forward to where things would go. He lived about an hour away with a schedule that did not permit us to spend much time together. I noticed that the level of connection we had did not compare to what I had with my ex-boyfriend, which I took as a sign that maybe he was not the right fit for me. The connection we started to build, I decided to end.

My ex-boyfriend and I would talk often. During one of our conversations, he asked if I was dating anyone new, and at the time, I was dating the new guy. I hesitated to confess, afraid that admitting I had taken an interest in someone else would result in him severing our connection, so I chose to deny it. As our friendship continued to develop, my ex and I started going out together; it almost felt like we never broke up. Eight months after this kind of relationship, we decided to get back together. Before we became official for the second time, I felt compelled to tell him about the guy I denied dating. I realized that not being honest when he asked could undermine his trust, and I desperately wanted to begin our relationship anew, with nothing to hide

After I explained to him that I was dishonest about dating someone while we were friends, he struggled to trust me again. This lack of trust bred issues early on in our second attempt at being together. I felt we had grown and learned to understand each other better this time around. Despite the complications with trusting me, he showed up every time I needed him and proved to be a constant in my life. Whenever I needed a solution to a problem, he was there.

Our relationship was headed towards marriage; however, it was still clear that we had some concerns that needed to be addressed. Arguments continued to happen, and trust remained fragile, which led to more disagreements. Conflicts would linger on for days, and our arguments became difficult to look past. The uneasiness I felt being with him brought up negative emotions, reminding me of similar challenges I faced in marriage. I was sad and frustrated, and it showed up in the relationship. I began to reconsider what I accepted as 'normal' and slowly began to pull away emotionally.

A serious relationship requires dedication to both personal and relational growth. It demands time, attention, and sacrifice. But at that point in my journey, I found myself pouring more energy into maintaining the relationship than into nurturing myself. The activities that once grounded and fulfilled me slowly became less of a priority. I fought to reclaim the progress I had made, but balancing my relationship and life was overwhelming.

Deep down, I knew I had to have a real 'come to Jesus' moment. I wanted to live a life of trusting God, so I decided to surrender my relationship with my boyfriend to Him, completely. I began to relinquish control and seek divine guidance on how to proceed with him; this meant that I had to become obedient to the Word of God so that I could discern the path He set forth for me. My therapist reminded me of a truth that might have taken me ages to remember during my relationship struggle. "Our past does not just vanish; it shapes how we perceive things now as well as how we will react to situations in the future." I then had an epiphany: life is not about carrying your past; it is about using it as a tool. My past became a lens I could look through to see what I would allow in my future. This revelation taught me to see my past traumas as a superpower. We can turn past experiences into present wisdom, steering our choices and helping us to set boundaries more effectively.

Navigating being in a relationship without losing myself was new territory for me. Since I began to care for myself in new ways, I could not lose myself again, so I had to bring this concern to the forefront in our relationship. It was not just difficult; it was uncomfortable because I felt like I was selfish for prioritizing my needs. I did not want to lose him. I knew that I wanted to stay together and that if it were up to me, this would be the man I would marry.

Our relationship continued to feel rocky, and I lost the feeling of security I once felt. I knew in that moment that what I wanted and what God wanted did not align, and I was utterly disappointed. I came to terms with the truth that I needed to invest more of my time in the areas of my life that were being compromised, but I felt uncertain about how to approach this subject within our relationship. Our relationship continued, but it had to look different because I recognized that I was no longer the same person. I had matured spiritually, and having him be a part of that became the most important aspect of our relationship. I asked him to join me in prayer and in reading the Bible, and he obliged.

One of the most pressing areas in our relationship that I felt convinced of was in our physical intimacy. We were sexually active, but I knew it was wrong because the Word teaches us that sex before marriage is immoral. After all, it goes against God's intended design for intimacy. The Bible teaches that sex was made to be enjoyed within the covenant of marriage. It is a total connection, mind, body, and soul. Every time we were intimate, I knew that we were not bonded under the covenant that Christ honors. I had an innate feeling that our relationship could not be blessed unless we did it God's way.

After several discussions, we agreed to wait until we were married. We began to pray together daily and started communication counseling to strengthen weak areas in our relationship. Our goal was for the counseling to help us understand each other's communication styles. We read the Word together, but that sometimes led to disagreements. Many times, he interpreted the Word in a way that made me question my faith. Still, I could clearly see his heart and his desire to make our relationship succeed, just as much as I wanted it to. I prayed fervently. I was in the Word daily, seeking the Lord's guidance. I fasted and drew closer to God, desperately seeking clarity about the direction my life should take. One weekend, I visited him while he was away for work. We went out for dinner the night I arrived, and everything seemed normal, except that feeling of uneasiness lingered.

When we got back to our hotel, I prayed before going to sleep. When I finally dozed off, I was suddenly woken up in the middle of the night. I began to pray again, pleading with God, *"Please, God, tell me what to do, please, tell me what you need me to do! Why do I feel so uneasy?"* Then, I heard the voice of God. It sounded like thunder echoing in my soul. It was audible. "Leave him!" His voice sent shivers down my spine; immediately, tears streamed down my face. This profound experience led to the difficult decision to part ways with my boyfriend again. I did not suddenly make this change; I held on. I met with my spiritual mentor and sister in Christ, who told me that I had to decide: listen to God or listen to myself. Though I trusted God, I felt shattered and confused, as if I had once more lost my way, but I chose to trust in my faithful Father.

Ending our relationship wasn't easy. He resisted, and deep down, I questioned myself—*why couldn't he be the one for me?* I began to realize that what had initially led me into this relationship was prioritizing what I believed was best for my life, rather than allowing God to be my guide. I pursued a relationship simply because I wanted one, living again by my own desires. Deep down, I knew I had not fully surrendered to God, though I claimed I had.

I began to experience a new sense of direction, one that came with peace rather than uneasiness. It did not make life without my boyfriend easy, though, and I missed him immensely. I leaned into my support system, friends, family, and my therapist to help me stay the course. I was so vulnerable to him that every time I had a problem, he was the first person I would think of calling, and sometimes I did. Surrendering this to God was hard. It required relinquishing control of the outcome of my relationship.

Those who know me personally are aware of my need to oversee and fix everything. However, this life of surrender, albeit challenging, was liberating. The Bible tells us that when Jesus ascended into heaven, he left us with the Holy Spirit to be our guide, to teach us, empower us, and bring us comfort. This kind of peace comes to those who choose to believe. Whenever I tried to guide myself, it only led to chaos. In this season, God showed me how He can break the handcuffs of the illusion of control and replace them with His peace. I recognize that my choices and the transformation I underwent might not resonate with everyone. I pray that by sharing my story, I can offer the hope of liberation through surrender to our Lord and Savior, Jesus Christ. Allow God to lead you, even if you don't fully understand the path that He's guiding you on. We can trust him because he is faithful. The Bible tells us that He's a God who cannot lie, and his promises will not return to us void. God led me to this point, right here on this page, to touch someone else's life so that they, too, can be set free. If my experiences can help even one person, then every obstacle I've faced thus far will have been worth it.

14

The Power of Surrender

Suffering can feel unbearable, and it is human nature to look for ways to ease the pain. After losing my siblings and my marriage, I was exhausted from the suffering. I believed in Jesus for healing, but in my healing journey, I felt like Jesus could use my help. I added the law of attraction and New Age practices into my spiritual life when infidelity forced its way in.

This New Age movement offered a way to become more spiritually in tune with myself. It taught me that focusing on positive feelings would help me create what I desired. This movement has a sneaky way of sounding true as it advocates holistic health, with a focus on self-healing and self-discovery. It provides a temporary solution to our problems. It was easy to embrace this belief because it resonated deeply with my search for immediate answers.

New-age practices, such as manifestation, the Law of Attraction, including crystals, and crystal healing, offered a fresh perspective on spiritual exploration. After everything I had been through, the traditional ways of following God were not working for me. There was something profoundly powerful about knowing that I could manipulate the outcome of my reality with just my thoughts, and I truly believed I had stumbled upon the answers to life's questions. Every day, this information would pull me in deeper as videos of this content populated my social media feed. I began to feel like life made more sense. I thought, *yes, of course, we were all put on this Earth to fulfill our desires and indulge ourselves! I must have been taught the wrong message all along!* Forget suffering; that was now for the simple-minded. I was determined to no longer be controlled by the teachings of the Holy Bible.

Following Jesus felt too hard. I wanted, instead, to self-soothe. Although I read and studied the Word of God, attended church, and prayed to God, I combined New Age with my faith in Jesus.

There was a part of me that knew this was not right. It felt ungodly, but I could not stop. I felt like having faith in Jesus alone was not enough. Following Jesus alone meant I had to confront parts of myself I could not let go of. It meant submitting to Biblical principles that, even when I did not fully understand or agree with them, brought discipline and structure into my life—something I knew I could never achieve on my own. It also meant living a sacrificial life of humility, forgiveness, and love. It meant putting aside my own desires to serve and help others. Letting go of New Age meant that I could no longer be in control and that I could no longer do life alone. I was challenged here because being vulnerable is an area I struggled with greatly.

This world is not our home; we are simply passing through. Walking with Jesus requires us to look beyond what we see—to focus on the bigger picture. As I came to understand this, I realized I needed to surrender every part of myself to Jesus so He could renew me from within.

Picking up my cross meant I had to be willing to die to the things that are against Him, letting go of the familiar 'me.'

I believed that because New Age spirituality felt easier, I had found a shortcut—a golden ticket—and that all I had to do was listen to myself to be led in the right direction. When I was journaling during my trials, I was doing more than just journaling. I was mapping out my present moments and my life's future as "the creator" of it, as if I had the power to control exactly how my life would unfold. I listened to a practitioner who would refer to themselves as "we," teaching that I was the creator of my own reality. They taught that I had the power to make things happen exactly the way I wanted, that I did not have to listen to anyone except my inner self, and that I could commit to all the things that made me feel good.

Adopting this belief allowed me to live in the now and to pardon my sins. It meant that I could live in what I perceived to be freedom. I was convinced that the only way I could show up as my "best self" and be truly happy was by making myself feel good. However, this led me down a path of self-destruction, compelling me to think much less of everyone else. I was convinced by listening to those who believed and practiced this that this information was true, and it became dangerous territory. I knew that I needed help to release this giant.

Adopting God's principles meant I had to learn to assert myself, which was something I cowered from doing since I was a young girl. I lost sight of moral and ethical principles, which led me to accept that if something resulted in harmony and positivity, it meant it was of God; however, that is not the truth. The overemphasis on pleasing 'self' pulled me away from accountability, God-centered community, and biblical wisdom that I could never receive from using meditation or crystals.

A tug of war ensued between surrendering and maintaining control. I lost so many battles by trying to control my life; there was a part of me that wanted the best of both worlds—to walk with Jesus' guidance but to be the one to lead. I knew these two realities could not coexist, so I continued to pray. During my divorce and second pregnancy, I realized I needed to let go of New Age practices completely. The conviction weighed heavily on me, and in my shame, I began by having an honest conversation with God. I asked him to restore me and to forgive me for accepting a belief system that led me away from the truth of God's Word. I also prayed to be selfless, and to find joy in making the world better, not just in self-improvement.

I plugged into my local church and a small group, and diligently sought opportunities to connect with other Christians. I kept asking God to help me think like him (renew my mind), to make me more selfless and loving (change my heart), and to make me thirst for the Word of God (gain wisdom, knowledge, and understanding) so that I could navigate this life successfully for the greater good of all (building the Kingdom of God).

As I became more intentional about building my relationship with God, I deleted and blocked new age information from my social media. I replaced it with sermons and teachings based on Scripture. I listened to the gospel, reminding me of Jesus' sacrifice on the cross for the sins of humanity. Christian author and entrepreneur Myron Golden once said, "The Bible is not just a book about religion; it is a book of principles, promises, patterns, parallels, precepts, practices, prayers, and prophecies." Hearing that shifted my perspective. It helped me draw closer to Jesus and live in a way that gives Him honor. After seeking Jesus, He restored my faith and showed me through His believers that He is a God of miracles. He also revealed in different circumstances in my life that He would take care of me, and that I could rest in him.

The Holy Bible contains moral and ethical principles designed to guide humanity in the way God intended for us to live. When I truly surrendered my life to Jesus and His teachings, I discovered the most selfless, loving, and patient version of myself. I still make mistakes, but through Him, I can bring my errors before God, humble myself, and find forgiveness. Living in a world shaped by sin, it's easy to fall into misinformation, but we can take this to Him and ask him to reveal the truth to us.

I want to reiterate that we are not meant to live this life in isolation. I struggled profoundly with being vulnerable, but growing in my faith meant I had to learn how to let myself be seen. Even though the Church is holy ground and a place of wonders, looking to people in the church alone to show me what Christ is like can lead to disappointment because the reality is that we are all humans, and humans are imperfect. I wanted to trust again. When I came into a relationship with God, I had to let go of all the past hurt that stemmed from being disappointed by people and situations that caused me distress. This was necessary to be in covenant with Jesus.

I discovered the true meaning of Salvation through class at church. I learned that there is nothing we can do to earn salvation; that this is a gift from God through Jesus. No one person deserves it more than another. We are God's children, created with a purpose and a gift to bring him glory. Ephesians 2:8 (NLT) says, "God saved you by his grace when you believed. And you can't take credit for this; it is a gift from God." We cannot make ourselves righteous enough in God's eyes, and no one can earn their way into Heaven by simply following God's laws. When we choose to follow Him, we receive forgiveness and salvation.

Our love and respect for Jesus inspires an internal transformation to obedience. We get to decide to follow His principles because He has graced us with the power of free will. The Bible says when we accept Jesus, we are invited to sit in God's presence, holy and unashamed. He's given us the ability to choose Him, willingly, not forcefully—that is the beauty of the gospel and the splendor of the depths of his love for humanity.

Jesus chose to accept his assignment, knowing that it would bring him to death. The Old Testament required the sacrifice of animals for the forgiveness of our sins, while Jesus' sacrifice would be once and for all. Despite the immense difficulty, Jesus surrendered to God's will, knowing that sacrificing Himself offered a far greater outcome than remaining alive while humanity remained lost. Matthew 26:39 (KJV) says, "And he went a little farther, and fell on his face, and prayed, saying, O my Father, if it be possible, let this cup pass from me: nevertheless, not as I will, but as thou wilt." A new covenant would be created by Jesus' sacrifice, making the blessings of the covenant accessible to all who believe. He asked for the cup of suffering to be passed from Him, yet He accepted it, knowing that He is humanity's second chance at freedom. If we believe that Jesus died on the cross for us, that he was raised from the dead, and is seated at the right hand of the Father, we are granted eternal life.

So much had happened in my life that tried to destroy me, but I continually pulled through, and I am here to tell you that Jesus is the reason. Challenges in life are unavoidable, regardless of your religious affiliation, race, ethnicity, or social status. Facing difficulties is a natural part of the human experience. While following God does not guarantee immunity from life's storms, placing ourselves in a position to listen to His guidance will help us defeat them, but this does not come without a battle. It was by deciding to remain steadfast in His Word and growing closer to spiritual mentors that I have become able to recognize forms of deception, become stable in my faith, and foster spiritual discernment. Our God is faithful and never fails to keep His promises. His love never fails, and he wants us all to be saved.

Grieving and going through tough times are never easy—it will hit us in every area of our lives, but these challenges are not just random struggles; they are part of God refining us for His purpose and glory. Life's trials equip us to help others, learn more about ourselves, and build resilience; they make us more like Jesus. If we run from adversity, the part of us that was created to make a real impact in the world cannot fully develop. God uses these moments to shape us into the people He intended us to be. Overcoming obstacles of grief and loss does not negate the pain you are experiencing; instead, it permits you to use the pain as fuel to become a light in the world. When you conquer the hardships you face, you begin to see the beauty of the life God has blessed you with and experience what many run from—the power of elevation that comes with walking in His strength.

15

From My Heart to Yours

Beloved Reader,

It is all too common to hide behind the facade of your own strength, convincing yourself and others that everything is fine. However, today, I want to remind you that it is necessary to be honest with where you are in your grief journey. It is okay to say, "I am not fine." To help you reach the place of healing, I want to share some steps I have discovered on my own path of healing in hopes of encouraging you to begin or further explore navigating the grief process.

Throughout my journey, I've realized that grief is not limited to losing a loved one. It is a complex emotion, stirring sadness, anger, guilt, or regret in response to the many changes life can bring. It is essential to acknowledge that your journey through it is unique. Embrace the full spectrum of your emotions. Do not permit anyone's idea of what is 'grief worthy' to dictate how you mourn. Allow yourself to grieve what matters to you and use that grief—not to weigh you down—but to fuel your growth, strengthen your spirit, and propel you forward in life.

I will leave you with six thought-provoking questions. These questions are designed to facilitate reflection, allowing you to begin navigating some of the complexities of your grief experience.

1. **What are the five stages of grief, and how are they impacting your life?**

2. How do you believe connecting with your faith can offer comfort and strength to you while you are experiencing trying times?

3. Are you open to seeking therapy? If not, what barriers exist that prevent you from considering it?

4. Why would it be important to prepare yourself for multiple losses in life (otherwise known as compound grief)?

5. How do you view the idea of setting new goals to transform your grief into purpose?

**6. Do you recognize the connection between grief and its physical and
emotional manifestations in your body? If so, how is it impacting your life?**

Remember, grieving is a personal journey, and there's no right or wrong way to go through it. However, if you are using methods of coping that are causing you harm, I urge you to seek help. Please, be gentle with yourself and try your best not to rush the process. Surround yourself with people who unconditionally support and love you. Lean on your faith, your community, and the strength God gives you to heal and grow.

You are not alone on this journey. I am here with you right now, and so are countless others who have faced their own losses. We can emerge from our pain stronger. Together, we can find healing, understanding, and ultimately, a renewed sense of purpose in life. Your story, your strength, and your healing can inspire others to find their way through the darkness and into the light. You are loved, valued, and your presence in this world makes a difference. Embrace your journey, and may it lead you to a place of peace and renewal. May you see that there truly is elevation in loss.

With faith and love,

Vanessa

Acknowledgements

There was a deep conviction within me that failing to share my story would prevent me from reaching the next phase in life God has envisioned for me. I firmly hold onto the belief that God transforms what was intended for harm into something beneficial, a sentiment echoed in Genesis 50:20 (KJV), "But as for you, ye thought evil against me; but God meant it unto good." Today, I stand as a new creation, a transformative work that came from accepting my identity in God. Trusting in his plan for my life is a true testament to His promise. To conclude, I wish to recognize the following:

To my daughter:

I love you with everything in me. A significant reason why I wrote my story was to contribute to your elevation when you need it most in life. I pray that you can use my story as a pillar of strength. You are destined for such amazing things, and I am so honored to be your mother.

To my mom and my brother:

Despite our family's reduction to half its size through the loss of our loved ones, I remain confident in God's faithfulness and believe the finest days lie ahead of us.

Mom, thank you for taking the time to answer my numerous questions, helping me piece my story together.

To my niece and nephews:

Our journey together has been incredibly life-changing. The connections I've shared with each of you have contributed significantly to my personal growth. I'm deeply grateful for the role you've played in my life. Thank you for allowing me into your world.

To my therapists and life coaches, and mentor:

I'm beyond appreciative of how you've pushed me to confront aspects of myself I desperately tried to avoid. Embarking on a journey of self-awareness alongside each of you has been crucial to my personal growth and development, and I cannot thank each of you enough. Mama T., thank you for your push, insight, and prophecy.

To Pastor Brent, Karla Garrard, and the wonderful community at In Focus Church:

The most crucial part of my healing journey began here. Being a part of, as Pastor Brent says, "a multi-generational, multi-ethnic church" that I believe is led by the power of the Holy Spirit, allows God to use us as his vessels to emulate God's love. Thank you for your love and dedication to Jesus.

To my family who rest in peace:

Your legacy will live on in the lives of our families, on and off these pages, forever: William and Marie Denise, Rene and Andre, Marie Lyvie, and Jean Marie Thomas Westerband.

Philocles and Philomene, Marie Therese, Nellie, Jacques, Jean Claude, Pierre Jacquelin, Jacques Dominique, Carline Andrieux, and Ludovic Arrieux.

To my dearest friends and extended family:

I am deeply grateful for your support through any of these moments.

To my best friend of over 30 years, for the years of shared memories, your love, support, and belief in me. Thank you for being part of this journey.

Each of you is an intricate part of my elevation.

I love you all

Appendix

Chapter 1

Yahoo is part of the Yahoo family of brands. (n.d.). https://ca.news.yahoo.com/the-stages-of-weight-loss-grief.html.

Chapter 2

Dilation and curettage (D&C) - Mayo Clinic. (2023, November 7). https://www.mayoclinic.org/tests-procedures/dilation-and-curettage/about/pac-20384910.

Chapter 4

1 Corinthians 13:4-7 (NIV). (n.d.). https://www.biblegateway.com/passage/?search=1%20Corinthians%2013%3A4-7&version=NIV; KJV.

Chapter 9

Tyrrell, P., Harberger, S., School, C., & Siddiqui, W. (2023, February 26). *Kubler-Ross Stages of Dying and Subsequent Models of Grief.* Stat Pearls - NCBI Bookshelf. https://www.ncbi.nlm.nih.gov/books/NBK507885/.

Chapter 14

Ephesians 2:8 (NLT). (n.d.). Bible Gateway. https://www.biblegateway.com/passage/?search=Ephesians%202%3A8&version=NIV.

Matthew 26:39 (NIV). (n.d.). Bible Gateway.

https://www.biblegateway.com/passage/?search=Matthew%2026&version=NIV.

New Age Philosophy explained: Your guide to New Age. (2022, May 8). Tiny Rituals.

https://tinyrituals.co/blogs/tiny-rituals/new-age-philosophy.

Proverbs 9:10 (NIV). (n.d.). Bible Gateway.

https://www.biblegateway.com/passage/?search=Proverbs%209%3A10&version=NIV.

Romans 12:2 (NIV). (n.d.). Bible Gateway.

https://www.biblegateway.com/passage/?search=Romans%2012%3A2&version=NIV.

What was the purpose of animal sacrifices in the Old Testament? (n.d.).

CompellingTruth.org. https://www.compellingtruth.org/animal-sacrifices.html.

Acknowledgement

Genesis 50:20 (KJV). (n.d.). Bible Gateway. https://www.biblegateway.com/passage/?search=genesis+50%3A20&version=KJV

www.ingramcontent.com/pod-product-compliance
Lightning Source LLC
Chambersburg PA
CBHW020938090426
42736CB00010B/1183